For Wally

First published 1987 by Walker Books Ltd
87 Vauxhall Walk, London SE11 5HJ

Special New Edition published 1997
This edition published 1998

2 4 6 8 10 9 7 5 3 1

Printed in Italy

British Library Cataloguing in Publication Data
A catalogue record for this book
is available from the British Library.

ISBN 0-7445-6166-3

WHERE'S WALLY?

MARTIN HANDFORD

WALKER BOOKS
AND SUBSIDIARIES
LONDON · BOSTON · SYDNEY

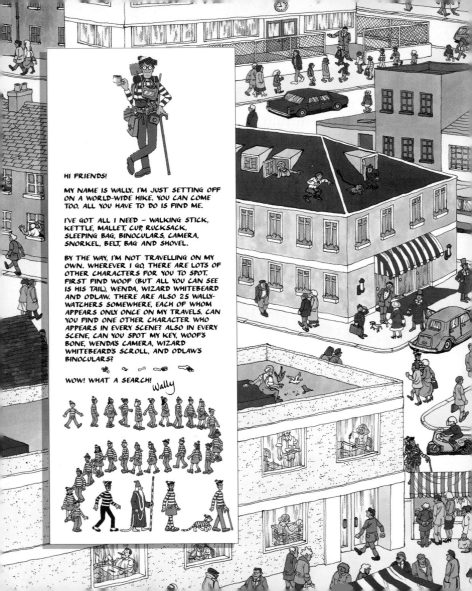

HI FRIENDS!

MY NAME IS WALLY. I'M JUST SETTING OFF
ON A WORLD-WIDE HIKE. YOU CAN COME
TOO. ALL YOU HAVE TO DO IS FIND ME.

I'VE GOT ALL I NEED – WALKING STICK,
KETTLE, MALLET, CUP, RUCKSACK,
SLEEPING BAG, BINOCULARS, CAMERA,
SNORKEL, BELT, BAG AND SHOVEL.

BY THE WAY, I'M NOT TRAVELLING ON MY
OWN. WHEREVER I GO, THERE ARE LOTS OF
OTHER CHARACTERS FOR YOU TO SPOT.
FIRST FIND WOOF (BUT ALL YOU CAN SEE
IS HIS TAIL), WENDA, WIZARD WHITEBEARD
AND ODLAW. THERE ARE ALSO 25 WALLY-
WATCHERS SOMEWHERE, EACH OF WHOM
APPEARS ONLY ONCE ON MY TRAVELS. CAN
YOU FIND ONE OTHER CHARACTER WHO
APPEARS IN EVERY SCENE? ALSO IN EVERY
SCENE, CAN YOU SPOT MY KEY, WOOF'S
BONE, WENDA'S CAMERA, WIZARD
WHITEBEARD'S SCROLL, AND ODLAW'S
BINOCULARS?

WOW! WHAT A SEARCH!

Wally

GREETINGS,
WALLY FOLLOWERS!
WOW, THE BEACH WAS
GREAT TODAY! I SAW
THIS GIRL STICK AN
ICE-CREAM IN HER
BROTHER'S FACE, AND
THERE WAS A SAND-
CASTLE WITH A REAL
KNIGHT IN ARMOUR
INSIDE! FANTASTIC!

Wally

TO:
WALLY FOLLOWERS,
HERE, THERE,
EVERYWHERE.

IT'S ME AGAIN, WALLY FOLKS!
SOME VERY STRANGE THINGS
WERE HAPPENING AT THE
AIRPORT THIS MORNING.
A HELICOPTER CHOPPED ALL
THE FLAGPOLES DOWN;
A SMUGGLER WAS CAUGHT
HIDING WATCHES IN HIS
BEARD; A HERD OF ELEPHANTS
WAS GETTING ONTO A JUMBO.
WEIRD!

Wally

TO:
WALLY FOLKS,
UNDER THE CARPET,
UNDER THE BED,
DOWN UNDER.

HOW-DE-DOO, WALLY SCHOLARS!
I'M CLEVER, AS YOU KNOW.
I GO TO MUSEUMS TO LEARN
THINGS. TODAY I FOUND OUT
ABOUT TICKLING THE TOES OF
A MAN IN THE STOCKS; ABOUT
KNOCKING DOWN A SUIT OF
ARMOUR; ABOUT THE
EGYPTIAN MUMMY'S BABY.
NOW THAT'S LEARNING!

Wally

TO:
WALLY SCHOLARS,
AT SCHOOL,
IN TROUBLE,
AGAIN.

WHERE'S
MUSEUM
WALLY?

WATCH IT, WALLY HUNTERS!
I'M AN ANIMAL LOVER, THAT'S
FOR SURE. I LOVE THAT HIPPO
WITH ITS ALARM CLOCK; THAT
LION HAVING ITS MANE COMBED;
THE HAT-EATING GIRAFFE; THE
OWLS IN SPECTACLES. GREAT!

Wally

TO:
WALLY HUNTERS,
NICE PLACE,
THE JUNGLE,
OUTSIDE.

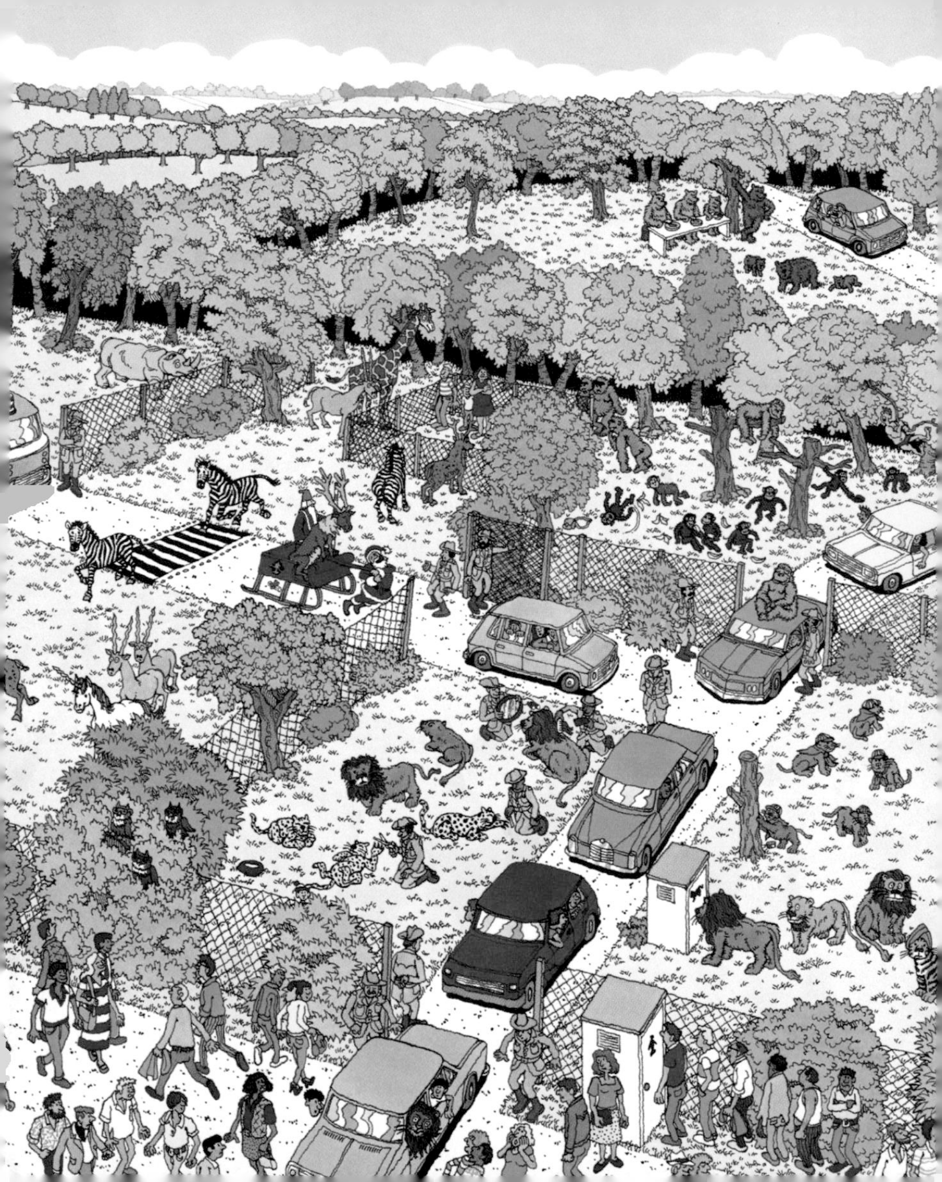

WOTCHA, WALLY-WATCHERS!
SAW SOME TRULY TERRIFIC
SIGHTS TODAY — SOMEONE
BURNING TROUSERS WITH
AN IRON; A LONG THIN MAN
WITH A LONG THIN TIE;
A GLOVE ATTACKING A MAN.
PHEW! INCREDIBLE!

Wally

TO:
WALLY-WATCHERS,
OVER THE MOON,
THE WILD WEST,
NOW.